T0011061

"Some struggles last a l
continue for the whole
to our Bible, this book
to pray for those in suffering, we are sure to find fresh and
important things to pray for."

Steve Midgley, Executive Director, Biblical Counselling UK

"This practical guide is such a needed tool in your prayer
belt as you look to comfort, encourage and walk alongside
a hurting brother or sister in Christ. Although you may not
have answers to give them, these prayers will equip you
with the words and wisdom to lay down the sorrow of a
fellow sufferer at the throne of God's grace. You'll likely
find your own heart encouraged along the way."

Sarah Walton, Author, *Hope When It Hurts*

"I love this series, and I love this volume. Helen has
done us a great favour by showing how we can pray
with biblical depth, hopefulness and clarity for suffering
saints. So many of my prayers for friends are simplistic
and lack the thoughtfulness that Helen provides.
Helen has shown me afresh how Christ-like confidence
enables me to pray more meaningfully and with greater
expectation. This book is a precious help."

Adrian Reynolds, Head of National Ministries, Fellowship
of Independent Evangelical Churches, UK

"Helen Thorne's heartfelt prayers are considered
and sensitive. Already, I have known their powerful
effectiveness as I have prayed through them, for
those I know who are suffering from grief, anxiety and
depression. My only negative is that this little book
wasn't written sooner. May it be used not only to touch
lives but to bring healing and wholeness."

Pauline Kennedy, Women's Ministry Development Officer
for the Presbyterian Church in Ireland

"Helen has brilliantly assembled a range of clear, biblical and pastoral prayers that we can pray for others—and for ourselves—in the midst of suffering. These prayers are arranged thematically and supply us with rich content as we seek God for our friends. They are neither triumphalistic nor wallowing in sadness but grounded in all that Scripture says about suffering and discipleship. I highly recommend this book for your own devotional life and as a pastoral resource."

Andy Mason, Vicar and Elder, St John's Church, Chelsea

"Caring for a suffering friend can paralyze us. We don't want to be like Job's friends and we don't want to come off as uncaring. We might not always know what to say, but we can pray. And in this short book, Helen Thorne provides practical, biblical, and honest prayers for us to use as we pray for and minister to our suffering friends."

Courtney Reissig, Author, *Teach Me to Feel*

"Abounding in the truth, hope and encouragement of Scripture, this engaging book is a valuable companion as you pray for suffering friends. Whether you're a seasoned prayer warrior or new to bringing heartbreaking situations to the Lord, you will find deep inspiration and wisdom to fuel your prayers. I will be praying these things for my friends and would be delighted to know that they were doing the same for me."

Pauline Williams, Congregation member, Roxeth Community Church, Harrow

"As someone who has had her fair share of suffering through illness, disability and family heartache, I want to say how wonderful it is to have this accessible guide which offers gospel truths and suggestions to love our brothers and sisters better!"

Nicola Thomas, Congregation member, Dundonald Church, Raynes Park

THINGS TO
5
PRAY

FOR A SUFFERING
FRIEND

HELEN THORNE

thegoodbook
COMPANY

5 things to pray for a suffering friend
Prayers that change things for friends or family who are walking through trials
© Helen Thorne, 2024
Series Editor: Carl Laferton

Published by:
The Good Book Company

thegoodbook.com | thegoodbook.co.uk
thegoodbook.com.au | thegoodbook.co.nz | thegoodbook.co.in

ISBN: 9781784989873 | JOB-007658 | Printed in Turkey

Design by André Parker

CONTENTS

INTRODUCTION

We live in a world full of suffering. Ever since our rebellion in Genesis 3, our hearts, our relationships, the very earth on which we tread has been broken. And that means life is painful. From the horrors of abuse to the struggles of anxiety, from the depths of grief to the grinding stresses and strains of work and home—we all know what it is to suffer. We all have friends who suffer too. We often wonder how to help; sometimes the only thing and the best thing we can do is to pray.

But how do we pray for them well?

In this short book, we explore a variety of ways to pray for a friend who is finding life hard.

As you read, it is worth bearing some things in mind:

> *Not every prayer will apply to every person—everyone's struggles are unique. Some will have short-term challenges, others will have chronic ones; some will have lots of support, others very little, some will be Christians, others won't be—*

and so we will want to pray differently for different friends.

- *Not every section in this book is comprehensive; there are many more ways we might pray than are listed here.*

- *Specific prayers are not linked to specific struggles—there are no distinct prayers for those with depression or those facing relational strife. The prayer points given can be applied to many different situations.*

- *The book is weighted towards (though not exclusively for) praying for believing friends whose struggles fall in the "commonly experienced" kind of category.*

But within these pages there are truths to hold on to and words to speak out to the Lord who is listening and loving both us and those we care about.

More than that, there is encouragement to keep praying without ceasing, confident that even when we cannot see hope or change or envision how things might possibly improve, we have a God whose kindness, grace, sovereignty and plans are deeper and more beautiful than we can ever begin to grasp.

As you begin, think widely about who you can pray for—think creatively about which prayers to pray for which person—and enjoy speaking to your Father who will, without doubt, answer in the ways he knows to be best.

HOW TO USE THIS GUIDE

This guide will help you to pray for your friend in 21 different areas of focus. There are five different things to pray for in each of the 21 areas, so you can use this book in a variety of ways.

- You can pray through a set of "five things" each day, over the course of three weeks, and then start again.

- You can take one of the prayer themes for the week and pray one point every day from Monday to Friday.

- Or you can dip in and out of it, as and when you want and need to pray for a particular area your friend is struggling with.

- There's also a space on each page for you to write in the names of specific situations, concerns, or people that you intend to remember in prayer.

Each prayer suggestion is based on a passage of the Bible, so you can be confident as you use this guide that you are praying great prayers—prayers that God wants you to pray, because they're based on his word.

THINGS TO
PRAY
5

PRAYING THAT YOUR FRIEND WILL...

EXPRESS
THEIR PAIN
TO GOD

PSALM 3

PRAYER POINTS:

_____

_____

_____

_____

Turning to the Lord in hard times is a privilege. And he loves to hear your voice. Pray that your friend will be able to...

 ## CALL OUT TO GOD

> *"LORD, how many are my foes! How many rise up against me!" (v 1)*

The Bible is full of lament—prayers that pour out the pain of hard times to the King of all ages. Each begin with addressing God, calling out to the one who knows and loves them. Pray that your friend will begin to speak to their Father, their King, their Saviour, their Friend.

TELL GOD ABOUT THEIR PAIN

> *"Many are saying of me, 'God will not deliver him.'" (v 2)*

God knows what is going on—we do not talk to him to inform him—but lament includes pouring out our hearts. As we do so it builds our relationship with him. Pray that your friend will feel able to share their honest emotions with God and know that he listens.

REMEMBER GOD'S NATURE

"But you, LORD, are a shield around me."
(v 3-6)

Sometimes lament feels futile, we wonder if God hears our words or if he cares. But the Bible's many psalms of lament show us that God loves for us to call out to him in this way. He is present with us and he loves to protect. Pray that your friend will know it is safe to turn to the Lord.

 ## ASK GOD FOR HELP

"Arise, LORD! Deliver me, my God!" (v 7)

Another integral part of lament is asking God for what we need. He does not always say "yes" to our requests—he answers in accordance with his will not ours—but he encourages us to ask and to ask with hearts full of trust. Pray that your friend will not forget to bring their needs before their Father today.

HAVE CONFIDENCE IN GOD

"From the Lord comes deliverance." (v 8)

God never promises quick relief, but he does promise to hold us fast. Lament is not just pouring out our hearts in the here and now but it spurs us to look towards a better future, whether that is in this world or the world to come. Pray that your friend will know God will be with them for the rest of their lives and lament with eyes that look forward to a time when they will suffer no more.

PRAYING THAT YOUR FRIEND WILL...

EXPRESS
THEIR PAIN
TO OTHERS

2 TIMOTHY 4:9-18

PRAYER POINTS:

_____

_____

_____

_____

We are designed to be interdependent with—not independent of—those around us. Pray that your friend will find the words to...

 EXPRESS THEIR STRUGGLES

"Do your best to come to me quickly, for Demas ... has deserted me." (v 9-10)

It can be easy to assume that we should stay quiet when life is hard—that we should just press on. Nothing could be further from the truth. The apostle Paul shows us that it's ok to express the pain we feel. When he was hurting, he said so. Pray that your friend will too.

 EXPRESS THEIR NEEDS

"When you come, bring the cloak ... and my scrolls, especially the parchments." (v 13)

When Paul was struggling in prison, he needed warmth and spiritual edification. So, he asked for what he needed. Pray that your friend will know there is no shame in asking for help from others. Pray that their friends will listen.

EXPRESS WARNINGS

*"Alexander the metalworker did me a
great deal of harm ... You too should be
on your guard against him." (v 14-15)*

Sometimes, when life hurts it is because an individual
or group is acting in ungodly ways. God is a God of
justice—he does not ask us to stay silent in the face
of sin. Pray that your friend will have the courage to
alert people to the danger others pose—and to do so
wisely, avoiding the pitfall of gossip.

 AVOID BITTERNESS

*"At my first defence ... everyone deserted
me. May it not be held against them." (v 16)*

It is good to express need in hardship; it is loving to
warn of danger, but believers aim to do those things
without seeking revenge. In the power of Christ, we
can want those who hurt us to be restored rather than
destroyed. Pray that your friend will shun bitterness.

 EXPRESS HURT WITH HOPE

*"But the Lord stood at my side and gave
me strength ... And I was delivered from
the lion's mouth." (v 17)*

Paul felt abandoned, hurt and cold. Yet he was able
to look back and see how God had worked in his life
in the past. God was faithful then—he will be in the
future too. Pray that your friend will speak out God's
track record of care.

PRAYING THAT YOUR FRIEND WILL...

TURN TO THE SUFFERING SERVANT

MARK 14:43-52

PRAYER POINTS:

_____

_____

_____

_____

When suffering hits, we sometimes assume God does not understand. We forget that Jesus has suffered immeasurably more than us. Pray that your friend will take comfort from knowing that Christ was...

OPPOSED

"A crowd armed with swords and clubs, sent from the chief priests, the teachers of the law, and the elders..." (v 43)

Jesus knows what it is to be hated. He is so good, so pure, so holy, and yet despised. When we are opposed, he gets it. Pray that your friend will speak boldly of their experience of opposition to the one who was hunted down with weapons.

BETRAYED

"Now the betrayer had arranged a signal with them: 'The one I kiss is the man.'" (v 44)

Being reviled by strangers is one thing, being wounded by a friend brings a new depth of pain. Pray that your friend will lament their experience along-side the one who knows that agony personally.

ACCUSED

"The men seized Jesus and arrested him."
(v 46)

Jesus had committed no sin. He suffered though he was completely innocent. We are not sinless, but we do still suffer in ways we do not deserve. Pray that your friend will find comfort in the one who knows what it is to be falsely accused.

 ## MISUNDERSTOOD

"'Am I leading a rebellion,' said Jesus, 'that you have come out with swords and clubs?'"
(v 48)

Jesus' mission was to save. His gospel is good news full of hope. Yet he was seen as a troublemaker, someone who would lead others astray. Pray that your friend will see the good news of Jesus, not misunderstand him. Pray that they would find strength in knowing he was misunderstood too.

 ## DESERTED

"Then everyone deserted him and fled."
(v 50)

There can be a deep loneliness in suffering—an isolation that piles on the pain. Pray that your friend will see that Jesus understands their sense of aloneness. But more than that, that by his abandonment, he was able to bring the salvation that means they never need to be alone. Pray that they will know his presence with them in the pain.

5 THINGS TO PRAY

PRAYING THAT YOUR FRIEND WILL...

PRAISE IN THE PIT

1 PETER 1:3-6

PRAYER POINTS:

_____

_____

_____

_____

Praise feels hard in the presence of pain but there are always good things for which to thank God. Pray that your friend will praise God...

 FOR HIS MERCY

"Praise be to the God and Father of our Lord Jesus Christ! In his great mercy..." (v 3)

The weight of sin is heavy, but those who are in Christ know the joy of having that weight removed. We do not face punishment but receive mercy. Even on the hardest of days, that wonderful liberation is worthy of our praise. Pray that your friend will revel in grace.

FOR NEW BIRTH

"He has given us new birth into a living hope through the resurrection of Jesus Christ from the dead." (v 3)

At the cross, Jesus did not just wash away the past, he changed the present too. Now, all who are in the risen Christ have a new life. Pray that your friend will thank God for the hope that this new beginning brings (or pray that they will come to know it).

FOR A SECURE INHERITANCE

*"… and into an inheritance that can never
perish, spoil or fade." (v 4)*

The future is transformed too. One day, there will be
perfection. Today, we can hold firm to that promise.
Pray that your friend will know there is no such thing as
an unhappy ending for those who are in Christ.

FOR HIS PROTECTION

*"… you, who through faith are shielded by
God's power until the coming of the salvation that is ready to be revealed in the
last time." (v 4-5)*

When life is painful, it can be hard to see how God is
protecting us, but we can never tell how much he is
protecting us from. He has promised to protect our
relationship with him, and he does not lie. Pray that
your friend will praise God for his protection.

AMID THEIR PAIN

*"In all this you greatly rejoice, though now
for a little while you may have had to
suffer grief in all kinds of trials." (v 6)*

In the pain of life there are hidden treasures. God
does not call us to be masochists who enjoy suffering,
but he does call us to be grace-hunters—people who
see glimpses of his glory in the mess of life and let our
hearts sing. Pray that your friend will be able to praise
God even when it is hard.

PRAYING THAT YOUR FRIEND WILL ...

CONTEND AGAINST THE DARKNESS

EPHESIANS 6:10-20

PRAYER POINTS:

_____

_____

_____

_____

We are in a spiritual battle. The only way to win is to follow our Lord as he fights evil. Pray that your friend will speak out against the darkness with the armour of God.

 BELT OF TRUTH

> *"Stand firm then, with the belt of truth buckled round your waist." (v 14)*

Truth matters. Satan is the father of lies. God is truth. Pray that your friend will believe what is true of God and believe what is true of themselves—and respond to hardship by speaking truth.

 BREASTPLATE OF RIGHTEOUSNESS

> *"… with the breastplate of righteousness in place." (v 14)*

Satan would love to use our suffering to encourage us to rebel and turn away from what is right. *Abandon God, he does not love you anymore* he whispers in our ears. Pray that your friend will ignore his twisted invitation and know that there is no better place to be than within Christ, the righteous one.

FEET FITTED WITH READINESS

"… and with your feet fitted with the readiness that comes from the gospel of peace." (v 15)

When life is hard, our passion for evangelism can ebb away. But suffering can be a wonderful context in which to testify to God's saving and sustaining work. We do not need to do something big; a quiet word can bring others hope. Pray that your friend will retain their passion for mission.

 ## SHIELD OF FAITH

"In addition to all this, take up the shield of faith, with which you can extinguish all the flaming arrows of the evil one." (v 16)

God does not protect us from everything hard. But just as an ancient army locked shields together so they could keep moving forward, as a church we can persevere in the mission he has called us to by encouraging each other in our faith. Pray that your friend will not be distracted by Satan's schemes.

 ## HELMET AND SWORD

"Take the helmet of salvation and the sword of the Spirit, which is the word of God." (v 17)

In suffering there is often doubt. It is good to ask God big questions but pray that your friend will turn to the Bible to find certainty. Pray that their big emotions would be processed under God's word.

THINGS TO 5 PRAY

PRAYING THAT YOUR FRIEND WILL ...

SEE GOD'S CHARACTER

LAMENTATIONS 3:22-27

PRAYER POINTS:

_____

_____

_____

_____

God is so good. Knowing this makes a difference.
Pray that your friend will see...

1 THE LORD'S LOVE

"Because of the LORD's great love we are
not consumed." (v 22)

There are times when life feels overwhelmingly bleak.
Jeremiah, the writer of Lamentations, knew that
feeling. Jerusalem had been destroyed, God's people
had been swept away and everything was beyond
awful. Yet God's love had not waned. Jeremiah was
able to see that God's love was what sustained his
people despite their rejection of him. Pray that your
friend will know the strength of that love too.

2 THE LORD'S COMPASSION

"For his compassions never fail." (v 22)

God's compassion is not often the first thing that
springs to mind when life is falling apart but Jeremiah
knew that even though his immediate circumstances
were crushing, God was bringing about something
good and kind. Pray that your friend will know God is
always compassionate, even on the hardest of days.

THE LORD'S STEADFASTNESS

"They are new every morning; great is your faithfulness." (v 23)

Jeremiah could have confidence in the Lord's character because he was not a remote, unpredictable God but a faithful God. He is the God who acts every day for our good. Pray that your friend will know his steadfastness today.

THE LORD'S SUFFICIENCY

"I say to myself, 'The LORD is my portion; therefore I will wait for him.'" (v 24)

There may be many things we want for our friends. Jeremiah doubtless wanted many things for his fellow-Israelites, but he reminded himself that God is the source of all he needed. The same is true for us. God promises to give us himself and he provides everything necessary. Pray that your friend will trust God for his provision.

THE LORD'S GOODNESS

"The LORD is good to those whose hope is in him, to the one who seeks him; it is good to wait quietly for the salvation of the LORD." (v 25-26)

Waiting is hard. Sometimes waiting feels impossible. However, waiting is part of God's good design. Pray that both they and you will develop patience as you wait for him to bring change. There is good ahead; it is worth waiting for.

THINGS TO
PRAY

PRAYING THAT YOUR FRIEND WILL...

DEVELOP
CONFIDENCE
IN GOD'S WAYS

HABAKKUK 3:2

PRAYER POINTS:

_____

_____

_____

_____

Pray that your friend would not waver in their convictions but develop fuller confidence in...

1 THE REPUTATION OF GOD

"LORD, I have heard of your fame."

Have you shown others how God has worked powerfully in the struggles you have faced? Your friend needs to hear this kind of encouragement about God's goodness in all circumstances from those around them. Pray that your friend will hear testimonies that display God's exemplary track record of acting wisely and well.

2 THE PROMISES OF GOD

"I stand in awe of your deeds, LORD."

Habakkuk was standing on the verge of disaster. Judah was about to be invaded and destroyed. But he could look back and see the history of God's continual rescue and redemption of his people. Pray that your friend will know the wonderful ways God has worked across the ages and see that he never breaks his promises.

THE POWER OF GOD

"Repeat them in our day."

God's actions are not small. Habakkuk knows that in leading his people, God sent plagues on their enemies, destroyed armies, miraculously provided food and parted the sea. Hundreds of years later, we saw Jesus control the weather, heal the sick and ultimately rise from the dead. Pray that your friend will know that same mightiness of God today through his Spirit.

 ## THE WILLINGNESS OF GOD

"In our time make them known."

Habakkuk shows us that even when life is hard and set to get harder, it is still possible to trust that God will work things together for the good of those who love him. If your friend loves Jesus, pray that they will persevere in prayer, confident in God's goodness not just for others but for them personally too.

THE MERCY OF GOD

"In wrath remember mercy."

Often, our suffering is not related to our sin. Sometimes, it is. When our friends are suffering because they are reaping the consequences of some waywardness or bad decision-making, it can be tempting to think that God will not act for their good, but he is a merciful God. Pray that they will know his tender grace and care and remember that his arms are always open to receive them again.

PRAYING THAT YOUR FRIEND WILL...

TRUST IN GOD'S FAITHFULNESS

PSALM 31:14-20

PRAYER POINTS:

_____

_____

_____

_____

Pray that your friend will keep trusting in...

HIS RELATIONSHIP

> *"But I trust in you, LORD; I say, 'You are my God.'" (v 14)*

God is not a distant God in a casual relationship with us. He is a covenant God—one who has promised to be our heavenly Father. Pray that your friend will know this is a solid and dependable relationship and will pursue and deepen that connection with him. Or, if they are not yet Christians, pray that they will come to know God in this way.

HIS TIMING

> *"My times are in your hands; deliver me from the hands of my enemies, from those who pursue me." (v 15)*

When the people near us are hurting, our instinct is to want things to be better soon. But God's timing is not our timing and he is holding all things together. Pray that your friend will know that his plans and purposes—sometimes deeply mysterious—often mean slow change rather than fast.

HIS LOVE

"Let your face shine on your servant; save me in your unfailing love." (v 16)

How precious it is to be a child of God. And that is what we are! Loved beyond measure, lavished with grace, blessed with every heavenly blessing. He could not love his children more. Pray that they will come to know more of God's perfect, active love.

HIS JUSTICE

"Let me not be put to shame, LORD, for I have cried out to you; but let the wicked be put to shame." (v 17)

People are cruel, words wound, lies abound and everything feels deeply unfair. If your friend is suffering due to the sin of others, pray that truth will shine out and injustice will be righted. His perfect nature will bring all things to ultimate justice in time.

HIS GENEROSITY

"How abundant are the good things that you have stored up for those who fear you, that you bestow in the sight of all, on those who take refuge in you." (v 19)

Sometimes we feel that God is withholding something from us. Like any good parent, God doesn't give us everything we want, but he is never mean. We have been given the best things in Christ. Pray that your friend will look forward to even more blessings.

THINGS TO

PRAY

5

PRAYING THAT YOUR FRIEND WILL...

GROW
THROUGH
GOD'S WORD

PSALM 119:33-36

PRAYER POINTS:

_____

_____

_____

_____

We have already prayed that our friend will read God's word to fight evil but we can want more than that. How wonderful for them to be transformed by God's word. Pray that your friend will be growing in...

1 STEADFASTNESS

"Teach me, LORD, the way of your decrees, that I may follow it to the end." (v 33)

Those who are suffering can find it hard to keep going. They may not have the energy for big Bible studies, but God's word still matters—within its pages are truth and beauty. Pray that your friend will turn to the Lord through his word and find the encouragement they need to carry on.

2 UNDERSTANDING

"Give me understanding, so that I may keep your law." (v 34)

We can all get muddled when life is difficult. The Bible can seem confusing and hard. But the Lord loves to help his children see the wonder that is contained in his word. Pray that they will hear what the Lord is saying and be surrounded by wise counsel.

WHOLEHEARTEDNESS

> *"Give me understanding, so that I may keep your law and obey it with all my heart." (v 34)*

While understanding the Bible is good, understanding is never enough on its own. We are called to love God's word and to live it out in every aspect of our lives. Pray that your friend will see how Scripture connects to their life and seek to serve the Lord with whatever capacity they have.

 DELIGHT

> *"Direct me in the path of your commands, for there I find delight." (v 35)*

The Bible should never be just duty, it is designed to be a joy. There will, of course, be moments when that joy becomes muted—pain can dull our ability to rejoice in anything. But you can pray that your friend will dig into the real beauty of God's word and find deep enjoyment in it.

 DESIRE FOR GOD'S WORD

> *"Turn my heart towards your statutes and not towards selfish gain." (v 36)*

Pray too that they won't get distracted from God's word. Pain shouts loudly; it encourages us to look inward to ourselves and outward to the world for fleeting comforts. Both are tempting but neither helps. Pray that your friend will desire to engage with God's word each day.

5 THINGS TO PRAY

PRAYING THAT YOUR FRIEND WILL...

HOLD ON TO THE PERFECTION TO COME

REVELATION 22:3-7

PRAYER POINTS:

_____

_____

_____

_____

Sometimes the Lord chooses not to heal. Sometimes this life brings no justice. The pain can be overwhelming but there is still hope. There is perfection to come. Pray that your friend will hold on to these truths.

1 BROKENNESS WILL GO

"No longer will there be any curse." (v 3)

The rebellion and curse of Genesis 3 lie behind all the suffering we experience now. The last book of the Bible reminds us that, one day, it will be no more. Curse gone; rebellion gone; all renewed. Pray that your friend will know that day is worth waiting for.

2 JESUS WILL BE WITH US

"The throne of God and of the Lamb will be in the city, and his servants will serve him." (v 3)

It is not primarily the absence of bad things that is going to make the new heavens and new earth so wonderful—it is the presence of Christ. In eternity, he will be at the centre and being with him will be our ultimate joy. Pray that your friend's enduring relationship with him will bring comfort and hope.

DARKNESS WILL GO

"There will be no more night. They will not need the light of a lamp or the light of the sun, for the Lord God will give them light." (v 5)

Without a curse, in the presence of the risen and ascended Christ, there can be no more suffering or sin. As Revelation 21:4 expands, we can look forward to no more death, mourning, crying or pain. What a delight that will be. Pray that your friend will know their departed Christian friends and family are safe in that perfection already.

VICTORY IS AHEAD

"And they will reign for ever and ever." (v 5)

With our battles against the world, the flesh and the devil over, the new heavens and new earth will be a place of victory. At present, we mess up and fall flat on our face time and again. But one day we will be able to look back and say, "In Christ, we won!" As your friend battles temptation, pray that they will be confident one day they will share in Jesus' victory.

PERFECTION IS COMING SOON

"Look, I am coming soon!" (v 7)

Jesus' return does not feel as if it is happening imminently. He has not forgotten though. He is not being tardy. The world is progressing towards that wonderful day. Pray that we will all be assured that restoration is on the way.

PRAYING THAT YOUR FRIEND WILL...

RECEIVE
COMFORT
FROM GOD

PSALM 145:8-14

PRAYER POINTS:

_____

_____

_____

_____

The weight of suffering can weigh heavily on our hearts. Pray that your friend will know comfort from...

GOD'S GRACE

"The Lord is gracious and compassionate, slow to anger and rich in love." (v 8)

When life is hard, we need not fear that God has rejected us as long as we are in Christ. Even when we are at fault in some way, he is patient and kind. He loves to console us. Pray that your friend will know God is caring for them—not condemning them—today.

BEING GOD'S WORKMANSHIP

"The Lord is good to all; he has compassion on all he has made." (v 9)

First and foremost, we are God's workmanship. He has designed and shaped us with purpose and precision. Of all creation, he chose to make us in his likeness. All believers are his precious children and living in his family! Pray that your friend will take comfort from their status as God's child—created by him and precious to him.

THE LORD'S MIGHT

"They tell of the glory of your kingdom and speak of your might." (v 11)

It is not very comforting when someone with no power to help us tells us that we can carry on. But there is huge comfort in being spurred on by the one whose might has broken the power of our own sin and the power of those who have sinned against us. Pray that your friend will see the difference the Lord's power makes in their life.

GOD'S ETERNAL PLANS

"... that all people may know of your mighty acts ... your dominion endures through all generations." (v 12-13)

God's plans are often mysterious. We play our part in them, but we do not necessarily have the big picture. That is because God is eternal. His purposes stretch far wider than our eyes can see. Pray that your friend will trust God's eternal plans even when they cannot understand why hard things happen.

GOD'S TENDERNESS

"The LORD upholds all who fall and lifts up all who are bowed down." (v 14)

The picture the psalmist paints is beautiful—a God who scoops up, consoles and restores those who have been broken by this fallen world. What tenderness; what love! Pray that your friend will know the gentle hand of the Lord carrying them right now.

PRAYING THAT YOUR FRIEND WILL...

RECEIVE
COMFORT
FROM OTHERS

ACTS 4:32-37

PRAYER POINTS:

_____

_____

_____

_____

Part of our purpose is to love each other well. Pray that your friend will be...

SUPPORTED BY A CHURCH

> *"All the believers were one in heart and mind." (v 32)*

There are many wonderful secular organisations and people in the community who can offer support—and we can be grateful for them—but pray that Christ-centred support will surround your friend too. And pray that the support will flow from unity in Christ.

BLESSED WITH GIFTS

> *"No one claimed that any of their possessions was their own, but they shared everything they had." (v 32)*

A local church is designed to be a place where practical needs are met. Whether it is offering money, making meals or mowing the lawn, there are so many opportunities to love each other well. Pray that your friend will receive practical help.

SURROUNDED BY GENEROSITY

"God's grace was so powerfully at work in them." (v 33)

The church is not just a place of giving but a place of giving generously. When the Lord is at work, hearts are stirred to give sacrificially. Pray that you will be one of those sacrificial givers and that your friend will know the privilege of giving what they can too.

 ## RECEIVING WHAT THEY NEED

"There was no needy person among them." (v 34-35)

The early church (when it was operating as it should) left none of its members in need. Can we grasp the enormity of that? None in need! Pray that your church will be ever more like that. Pray that your friend will be able to say, "The church supplied my needs".

 ## ENCOURAGED

"Barnabas (which means 'son of encouragement'), sold a field he owned and brought the money and put it at the apostles' feet." (v 36-37)

It is possible to give in ways that encourage or in ways that do not. Giving in a patronising or cold way brings little comfort. Giving in love, for the glory of God, brings huge comfort. Pray that your friend's needs will be met by people whose hearts are eager to encourage with their words and actions, rather than just going through the motions.

PRAYING THAT YOUR FRIEND WILL...

GRASP HOPE

ROMANS 15:13

PRAYER POINTS:

_____

_____

_____

_____

We have prayed for hope, joy and power to be present in your friend's life. Now we pray for how they work together. Pray that your friend will hold firm to…

 HOPE

"May the God of hope fill you..."

God does not just give us hope—he is himself the source of hope. In him there is love, strength, purpose, help, blessing and so much more. Without him, there is nothing good. Pray that your friend will know there is hope, because there is God.

 JOY

"May the God of hope fill you with all joy."

Hope spills over into other aspects of our lives. If we have no hope for the future, we have nothing to rejoice in. But when we possess hope, our hearts are lightened by faith in God's promises and our joy comes from a source that will not run out. Pray that your friend will know the practical outworking of hope—a life of joy, even through sorrow.

PEACE

> *"May the God of hope fill you with all joy and peace."*

Hope brings peace too. The more we hope in God, the more we see him as loving and strong, the less we will fret about the complexities we face. We never forget the hard things, but they do not need to dominate our minds. Pray that your friend will know peace.

 THEIR TRUST IN GOD

> *"May the God of hope fill you with all joy and peace as you trust in him."*

As we see God more clearly—and taste the benefits of living in him—we grow in our trust. When life is hard, we need someone to follow. Bit by bit, we can come to know there is no one better to rely on than the Lord. Pray that your friend will grow in trust today.

 THE SPIRIT'S POWER

> *"May the God of hope fill you with all joy and peace as you trust in him, so that you may overflow with hope by the power of the Holy Spirit."*

There are days when it can seem too hard to even get out of bed. And there are days when it is good to rest. But we will always have the strength to do what the Lord asks of us because he is at work in us. Pray that your friend will rely more and more on the power of the Holy Spirit to give them strength.

THINGS TO
PRAY
5

PRAYING THAT YOUR FRIEND WILL...

KNOW THEIR IDENTITY IN CHRIST

EPHESIANS 1:3-14

PRAYER POINTS:

_____

_____

_____

_____

Hard experiences skew the way we see ourselves. Pray that your friend will know they are...

BLESSED

"Praise be to the God and Father of our Lord Jesus Christ, who has blessed us in the heavenly realms with every spiritual blessing in Christ." (v 3)

Life does not always feel like a blessing but if we are in Christ, we have been given so much. Eternally, everything is sorted. Here and now, there is hope and help. Pray that your friend will be able to adopt such a heavenly perspective on their lives.

CHOSEN

"For he chose us in him before the creation of the world to be holy and blameless in his sight." (v 4)

One of the great privileges of the Christian life is knowing we have been hand-picked by the King of creation to join his family. Our salvation is no accident. Pray that your friend will know that privilege.

REDEEMED

> *"In him we have redemption through his blood, the forgiveness of sins." (v 7)*

Being redeemed means to be bought back at a price. Jesus was willing to pay with his very life for our salvation! Such amazing grace. And that purchase was once and for all time. No more payment is needed. Pray that your friend will be assured that their salvation is secure and in Christ their value is priceless.

 FOR HIS GLORY

> *"... predestined ... in order that we, who were the first to put our hope in Christ, might be for the praise of his glory." (v 11-12)*

All Christians have a purpose. We are designed to be people who show how wonderful God is. That does not require us to be shiny and sorted but rather to show how his grace transforms our lives, in every circumstance. Pray that your friend will grasp that call.

 SEALED WITH THE SPIRIT

> *"When you believed, you were marked in him with a seal, the promised Holy Spirit, who is a deposit guaranteeing our inheritance." (v 13-14)*

The Spirit of God himself lives inside all who believe. He guarantees that one day we will know the full wonder of being a child of God. Pray that your friend will be fully confident in their eternal identity and know that their experiences on this earth do not define them.

THINGS TO
5
PRAY

PRAYING THAT YOUR FRIEND WILL...

EMBRACE PHYSICAL REST

1 KINGS 19:5-9

PRAYER POINTS:

_____

_____

_____

_____

God has made us with a physical body and soul. Pray that your friend will have...

GOOD REST

"Then he lay down under the bush and fell asleep." (v 5)

Elijah was a prophet who had seen God work extraordinary acts. He had experienced terrifying opposition. And now he was exhausted and feeling as if he could not go on. What does God do? Tell him to get up? Ask him to persevere? Not yet! First, he encourages rest. Pray that your friend will find rest too.

NUTRITIOUS FOOD & DRINK

"All at once an angel touched him and said, 'Get up and eat.'" (v 5)

Food is one of God's many good gifts to us. We need it if we are to live for him well. Our bodies will always function better if they are given the fuel they need. Pray that your friend will eat well. And if needed pray that people will provide them with food to eat so they do not have to prepare it themselves.

REPEATED REST

> *"He ate and drank and then lay down again." (v 6)*

Elijah rested more than once. When life is hard, we need to rest again and again! It is so tempting to try to press on when we should be slowing down. Pray that your friend will keep on resting when they need to—without guilt—and that others will be able to step in to do the things they cannot.

STRENGTH

> *"Strengthened by that food, he travelled for forty days and forty nights until he reached Horeb, the mountain of God." (v 8)*

None of us cope well when we are running on empty. We need the capacity to persevere in the lives God has called us to. Pray that your friend will have the physical and mental strength to carry on.

PHYSICAL PROTECTION

> *"There he went into a cave and spent the night." (v 9)*

Sometimes we need protection. Not just spiritual protection but physical protection too. That might mean getting support from the police, the housing department, a hospital, the law courts or something else. There is no shame in seeking physical safety. If your friend needs it, pray that they will find safe shelter.

PRAYING THAT YOUR FRIEND WILL...

EXPERIENCE HEALING

LUKE 18:35-43

PRAYER POINTS:

_____

_____

_____

_____

Jesus is the ultimate healer. Healing is often physical, but it encompasses the hurts of our heart too. Like many who met Jesus, pray that your friend will...

 KNOW THE HEALER IS CLOSE

"As Jesus approached Jericho, a blind man was sitting by the roadside begging. When he heard the crowd going by, he asked what was happening. They told him, 'Jesus of Nazareth is passing by.'" (v 35-36)

When we have been suffering a long time, we can start to think that Jesus is not interested in healing anymore—but God is still the same God. Thank God for his power to heal your friend and pray that this healing power would be at work in them now.

 CALL OUT WITH CONFIDENCE

"He called out, 'Jesus, Son of David, have mercy on me!'" (v 38)

The man born blind did not hesitate to ask Jesus for mercy. He wanted help. He needed help. So do we. Pray that your friend will not stop asking God to act, and will seek medical wisdom too.

NOT BE DETERRED

> *"Those who led the way rebuked him and told him to be quiet, but he shouted all the more." (v 39)*

There are those who think that asking for healing is wrong. There may be moments when we choose not to pray publicly for physical healing out of respect for an individual's wishes, but the Bible encourages us to keep praying for God's will. Pray that your friend will not get distracted by those who encourage them to stop praying.

 ## PRAY SPECIFICALLY

> *"Jesus asked him, 'What do you want me to do for you?' 'Lord, I want to see' he replied." (v 41)*

Jesus' mercy is not dependent on us finding the right words to say—but if we want him to act, it is good to be specific about what we want him to do. Pray that your friend will articulate what they need.

 ## KNOW WHOLENESS IN TIME

> *"Jesus said to him, 'Receive your sight; your faith has healed you.' Immediately he received his sight and followed Jesus, praising God." (v 42-43)*

Sometimes Jesus heals quickly, sometimes slowly—sometimes not until the new heavens and new earth. But he will heal. Pray that your friend will thank God each time a measure of healing is received.

PRAYING THAT YOUR FRIEND WILL...

COURAGEOUSLY PERSEVERE

HEBREWS 12:1-3

PRAYER POINTS:

_____

_____

_____

_____

Hardship is often not short-lived, but he will give us the means to keep going. Pray that your friend will…

 ## BE INSPIRED BY OTHERS

"Therefore, since we are surrounded by such a great cloud of witnesses, let us throw off everything that hinders and the sin that so easily entangles." (v 1)

The saints in heaven, and even the saints around us today, can show that perseverance is possible. They lived lives of repentance and faith in the messiness of life—we can too, in God's strength. Pray that your friend will find good role-models and follow in the faithful footsteps of those who have gone before.

PRESS ON WHOLEHEARTEDLY

"And let us run with perseverance." (v 1)

Sometimes all we need to do is take the next small step forward. God does not demand great acts of heroism from us, just a commitment to trust him in this moment and put one foot in front of the other. Pray that your friend will keep on keeping on—moment by moment, day by day.

KNOW A PATH IS PREPARED

"Let us run ... the race marked out for us."
(v 1)

Pain is to be expected in this life—Jesus himself promised we would not avoid it (John 16:33). So, in times of trouble, we are not treading strange and uncharted territory but are following God's purposes. Pray that your friend won't be surprised by suffering but will be comforted by knowing there is a route through pain to glory.

 ### FIX THEIR EYES ON JESUS

"... fixing our eyes on Jesus, the pioneer
and perfecter of faith." (v 2)

Look up! That is the key to perseverance. Not looking in—to our pain. Not looking down —in despair. But up—up to the King, the Lord, the Saviour, the one who has gone before us and who will use hard things to make our faith complete. Pray that your friend will keep their eyes looking upwards to Jesus.

 ### DWELL ON JESUS' EXAMPLE

"Consider him who endured such opposi-
tion from sinners, so that you will not
grow weary and lose heart." (v 3)

Jesus completed the race. He went through more suffering than we can imagine. He endured far more than will ever be asked of us. And he enables us to face trials too. Pray that your friend will see Jesus' life and death and be encouraged about their own lives.

PRAYING THAT YOUR FRIEND WILL...

FORGIVE THOSE WHO WOUND

COLOSSIANS 3:1 & 12-14

PRAYER POINTS:

_____

_____

_____

_____

Forgiveness is complex. Pray that your friend will...

KNOW FORGIVENESS

"Since, then, you have been raised with Christ..." (v 1)

Before we can forgive others, we need to know the wonder of being forgiven. The Lord has blessed us so deeply; washed us whiter than snow and given us new life. Pray that your friend will grasp the depths of God's grace and mercy and the privilege of new life—and repent where that is necessary.

DESIRE WHAT GOD DESIRES

"Set your hearts on things above, where Christ is, seated at the right hand of God." (v 1)

Most of us do not naturally feel forgiving towards those who have hurt us. We would much prefer to ignore them or seek revenge. But the Christian life is about wanting what God wants for our relationships. That does not mean ignoring justice, but it does mean pursuing love. Pray that your friend's will aligns with the Lord's.

DEVELOP A KIND ATTITUDE

*"Clothe yourselves with compassion, kind-
ness, humility, gentleness and patience."*
(v 12)

Even in the face of suffering, we are called to be kind.
We can seek justice kindly; speak the truth kindly;
rebuke kindly; forgive kindly. Pray that kindness,
compassion and gentleness will pour out through
your friend's words.

 BEAR WITH MINOR OFFENCES

"Bear with each other." (v 13)

Some things do not need to be discussed. Some
minor indiscretions can be allowed to slide. No one
benefits from having every little sin pointed out, every
time it is committed, or every mistake analysed in full.
Pray that your friend will be able to let go of some of
the smaller hurts.

 FORGIVE THOSE WHO REPENT

*"Forgive one another ... forgive as the
Lord forgave you." (v 13)*

Pray too that your friend will have a right pursuit of
forgiveness. Forgiving others should be our default
desire, but we forgive like Jesus—the one who, at the
cross, lavished sinners with grace and yet calls people
to repent. Forgiveness and justice go hand in hand.
Pray that your friend will find healing and a burden
lifted as they forgive today.

THINGS TO PRAY 5

PRAYING THAT YOUR FRIEND WILL...

DISPLAY FRUIT

GALATIANS 5:22-23

PRAYER POINTS:

_____

_____

_____

_____

Suffering can harden our hearts, but it can also be a time of great fruitfulness in our character and relationships. Pray that your friend will develop increasing...

 LOVE

> *"The fruit of the Spirit is love." (v 22)*

Sometimes suffering can give us a greater understanding of God's love. We understand a small glimpse of what Jesus went through on our behalf because of his great love for us. Experiencing pain can also build our empathy towards others. Pray that even when they are overwhelmed by their own difficulties, your friend will be pleased to love others well.

 JOY AND PEACE

> *"The fruit of the Spirit is love, joy, peace..."*
> *(v 22)*

As well as knowing peace for ourselves, peace can be a defining characteristic of the way we relate to other people. Rather than contributing to any discord, pray that your friend will be at peace with the people around them (as far as that is possible).

KINDNESS AND GENTLENESS

> *"The fruit of the Spirit is ... kindness, goodness, faithfulness, gentleness and self-control." (v 22-23)*

The temptation to blame or lash out can be strong, even when others have done us no wrong. We get exasperated and tend to pass on our pain. Pray that your friend will be gentle with the friends and family who may be caring for them.

 ## GOODNESS AND FAITHFULNESS

> *"The fruit of the Spirit is ... goodness, faithfulness..." (v 22)*

Christians are called to shine as a light in dark places—to be people who radiate goodness, even when few others do. We will not always live up to that call, but you can pray that your friend will desire to be known as good. And will repent on those occasions when they are not.

FORBEARANCE AND SELF-CONTROL

> *"The fruit of the Spirit is ... forbearance ... and self-control." (v 22-23)*

It is so easy to find comfort in excess: too much food, too much social media, too much alcohol, too much work. God calls us to something better: to keep going through the pain with him, without turning to idols that offer hollow hope. Pray that your friend will exercise self-control and find solace in the Holy Spirit.

PRAYING THAT YOUR FRIEND WILL...

GROW IN FAITH

1 PETER 1:6-9

PRAYER POINTS:

_____

_____

_____

_____

Our God never wastes suffering. It is fertile ground for faith to mature. Pray that your friend will develop...

A BEAUTIFUL FAITH

"You may have had to suffer grief in all kinds of trials. These have come so that the proven genuineness of your faith ... may result in praise, glory and honour when Jesus is revealed." (v 6-7)

Sometimes suffering can be the context in which we discover how much we believe in Christ. If your friend is a believer, thank God for their faith in him.

A REFINED FAITH

"Your faith—of greater worth than gold, which perishes even though refined by fire—may result in praise." (v 7)

God's desire is for us to be holy—to be like Christ. Suffering often reveals our wayward desires and gives us an opportunity to repent of those things that distract us from faith. Pray that God would grow a stronger faith in your friend's life through repentance.

A LOVE FOR CHRIST

"Though you have not seen him, you love him." (v 8)

Sometimes we might wish God would appear to us in some kind of physical way—we think that might give us more strength to persevere. But we can love him even while we cannot see him face to face. We have the privilege of living in a time after Jesus has walked on earth in physical form, where we can read about the wonderful nature of his words and deeds in the Gospels. Pray that your friend will have an ever-deepening love for Jesus.

A JOYFUL BELIEF

"And even though you do not see him now, you believe in him and are filled with an inexpressible and glorious joy." (v 8)

Belief and joy go hand in hand. Joy does not mean ignoring the pain, but it does mean turning our eyes to see the wonder of our salvation. Pray that your friend will believe more fully and in turn find more joy.

A FRUITFUL SALVATION

"For you are receiving the end result of your faith, the salvation of your souls." (v 9)

There are eternal benefits to suffering. That fact does not make suffering good, but it can make it fruitful. Pray that your friend will know their reward is getting closer with each passing day of hardship.

PRAYING THAT YOUR FRIEND WILL...

TESTIFY TO THE GOODNESS OF GOD

JOHN 4:1-39

PRAYER POINTS:

_____

_____

_____

_____

Even the most broken lives can be restored. Pray that your friend will know the wonder of...

 ## GOD DRAWING NEAR

> *"When a Samaritan woman came to draw water, Jesus said to her, 'Will you give me a drink?'" (v 7)*

Jesus moves towards the hurting and the marginalised. Pray that your friend will know that God is drawing close to them, with deep compassion.

 ## ACCESS TO LIVING WATER

> *"Jesus answered, 'Everyone who drinks this water will be thirsty again, but whoever drinks the water I give them will never thirst. Indeed, the water I give them will become in them a spring of water welling up to eternal life.'" (v 13-14)*

How incredible to know the satisfaction and life that only Jesus can bring. Pray that your friend will turn to Jesus for all they need and be content in his provision of living water.

3 BEING TRULY KNOWN

*"'The fact is, you have had five husbands'
... 'Sir,' the woman said, 'I can see that
you are a prophet.'" (v 18-19)*

Sometimes we do not like the idea of God knowing us completely. After all, he gets to see all the suffering and all the sin, and it is not a pretty sight. But being fully known and fully loved by Jesus is safe and it can lead to transformation. Pray that your friend will love being known by their Saviour.

4 WORSHIP IN SPIRIT & TRUTH

*"Yet a time is coming and has now come
when the true worshippers will worship
the Father in the Spirit and in truth." (v 23)*

There is true religion and there is false. Pray that your friend seeks refuge in Jesus—nowhere else. Pray for the Spirit's work in them, that they would overflow with love and worship for Jesus and his word.

5 SAYING COME AND SEE

*"Many of the Samaritans from that town be-
lieved in [Jesus] because of the woman's
testimony." (v 39)*

Good can come from suffering, not only in our own lives, but in the community around us. Pray that through their hardship, your friend will be able to share the hope they have in Jesus; that they will have the privilege of seeing others come to Christ.

EXPLORE THE WHOLE SERIES

"A THOUGHT-PROVOKING, VISION-EXPANDING, PRAYER-STIMULATING TOOL. SIMPLE, BUT BRILLIANT."

SINCLAIR FERGUSON

thegoodbook
COMPANY

BIBLICAL | RELEVANT | ACCESSIBLE

At The Good Book Company, we are dedicated to helping Christians and local churches grow. We believe that God's growth process always starts with hearing clearly what he has said to us through his timeless word—the Bible.

Ever since we opened our doors in 1991, we have been striving to produce Bible-based resources that bring glory to God. We have grown to become an international provider of user-friendly resources to the Christian community, with believers of all backgrounds and denominations using our books, Bible studies, devotionals, evangelistic resources, and DVD-based courses.

We want to equip ordinary Christians to live for Christ day by day, and churches to grow in their knowledge of God, their love for one another, and the effectiveness of their outreach.

Call us for a discussion of your needs or visit one of our local websites for more information on the resources and services we provide.

Your friends at The Good Book Company

thegoodbook.com | thegoodbook.co.uk
thegoodbook.com.au | thegoodbook.co.nz
thegoodbook.co.in